BUDDHISM

BULLET GUIDE

Paul Oliver

Hodder Education, 338 Euston Road, London NW1 3BH

Hodder Education is an Hachette UK company

First published in UK 2011 by Hodder Education

This edition published 2011

Copyright © 2011 Paul Oliver

The moral rights of the author have been asserted

Database right Hodder Education (makers)

Artworks (internal and cover): Peter Lubach
Cover concept design: Two Associates

British Library Cataloguing in Publication Data: a catalogue record for this title is available from the British Library.

10 9 8 7 6 5 4 3 2 1

The publisher has used its best endeavours to ensure that any website addresses referred to in this book are correct and active at the time of going to press. However, the publisher and the author have no responsibility for the websites and can make no guarantee that a site will remain live or that the content will remain relevant, decent or appropriate.

The publisher has made every effort to mark as such all words which it believes to be trademarks. The publisher should also like to make it clear that the presence of a word in the book, whether marked or unmarked, in no way affects its legal status as a trademark.

Every reasonable effort has been made by the publisher to trace the copyright holders of material in this book. Any errors or omissions should be notified in writing to the publisher, who will endeavour to rectify the situation for any reprints and future editions.

Hachette UK's policy is to use papers that are natural, renewable and recyclable products and made from wood grown in sustainable forests. The logging and manufacturing processes are expected to conform to the environmental regulations of the country of origin.

www.hoddereducation.co.uk

Typeset by Stephen Rowling/Springworks

Printed in Spain

Contents

About the author

Dr Paul Oliver is a lecturer in Religious Studies at the University of Huddersfield. He specializes in eastern religions. He currently teaches courses on the religions of China and Japan, and on techniques of research applied to religious studies. He has travelled extensively throughout the Far East.

His publications include books in the areas of philosophy, education and religious studies, and have been translated into seven languages. His book *World Faiths: An Introduction* (in the Teach Yourself series) is published by Hodder Education and is now in its fourth edition.

Introduction

Buddhism is a religion and philosophy that was established first in India and subsequently spread to Asia. In its original form it has **no concept of a God** or divine being, and this may be why it has become popular recently in the secularly oriented West.

The original **Buddha**, or 'enlightened one', was an ordinary human being who developed and advocated techniques to analyse and reduce human suffering. He suggested that we should reflect on **the nature of suffering**, arguing that we suffer less because of unpleasant events but because of our reaction to them. He also taught that we should recognize the **impermanence** of existence, so that we can learn to become less attached to things.

Buddha also argued that human beings do not possess any unchanging entity within them, such as a soul. Since there was **no permanent 'self'**, we could learn to be less obsessed with ourselves, and through **meditation** aim to achieve **enlightenment**.

1 The life of the Buddha

Who was the Buddha?

The person we call the Buddha was born about 500 years before Christ in what is now Nepal. His birth name was **Siddhartha Gautama**. For most of his life he was a wandering spiritual teacher.

He came to understand the nature and problems of human existence from which he developed the principles of his teaching. He became known as the Buddha, or 'the enlightened one'. This was the origin of the term **Buddhism**.

The Buddha means 'the enlightened one'
....

This chapter describes Siddhartha's life. Here are the key points:

* Siddhartha was born in the town of **Lumbini** in the small state of Kapilvastu.
* His father, **Suddhodana**, ruled this state.
* Siddhartha was married at about the age of 16 and led an affluent life.
* At about the age of 29, he explored the area beyond the palace.
* He saw people who were old or ill, or who had died.
* He wanted to understand the **problems of human existence**.
* He decided to leave the palace and lead **a solitary, religious life**, finally teaching his ideas.

A sheltered life

It would have been difficult for Siddhartha to leave his family. He had a son, and was expected to succeed his father as king.

> Siddhartha had led a sheltered life in the palace, and must have been moved to encounter the suffering inherent in human existence.

● As a young man Siddhartha lived in the lap of luxury.

* Siddhartha had an overwhelming need to try to understand the **nature of suffering**, illness and death.
* Above all he wanted to give people ways of coping better with the suffering in their lives.

Upon leaving the palace, Siddhartha knew that he wanted to relieve the suffering of people, but how was he to achieve this?

* Siddhartha practised forms of **yoga** alongside several different mendicants, but felt he was not on the right path.
* He met five other wandering holy men, and **fasted** until he was extremely thin.

'Siddhartha practised such self-deprivations as suppression of breath and extended fasting.'

T. J. McDonald

* He may well have died had not a young girl from a nearby village brought him some rice to eat.
* Siddhartha decided to turn his back on such extreme practices, and find **his own way** to enlightenment.

Siddhartha's spiritual search

The Middle Way

When Siddhartha realized that a spiritual search based upon **extreme practices** would be counter-productive, he decided that he needed to meditate in order to understand the nature of existence. This was the 'Middle Way' that he adopted, which avoided extremes of behaviour.

He sat under a tree at **Bodh Gaya** in northern India, setting out to meditate until he found the truth. This tree became known as the **Bodhi** tree.

After many days meditating, he came to understand the nature of human suffering, and how it could be reduced. After some reflection, he decided to pass on to all human beings the **dharma** (or **dhamma**), or teaching, which he had discovered.

'When the student is ready, the master appears.'

Buddhist proverb

Siddhartha and the holy men

The Buddha walked to the holy city of **Benares** on the River Ganges. There he explained his teachings for the first time. He spoke to the five holy men whom he had known earlier.

The holy men thought that Siddhartha had given up his search for enlightenment, but were impressed by his teachings and became his first disciples. This is when he first became known as the 'enlightened one', or the Buddha.

The essence of his teaching can be summed up as the **Four Noble Truths**, which concern the way to eliminate suffering in life.

● 'This is the pathway to end suffering.'

The foundation of the sangha

The five holy men became, with the Buddha himself, the foundation of the **sangha**.

* On one level, this is the community of monks and nuns who have taken the vows required for monastic living.
* In a wider context, the sangha can also be considered to include all Buddhist laypeople who support monks and nuns living in monasteries. Laypeople donate food and money to the monastery, and try to live their lives according to Buddhist principles.
* Among academics and Buddhist historians, there is debate about the most accurate definition of the sangha.

The Buddha, the dharma (or Buddhist teachings) and the sangha of monks and nuns became one of the building blocks of Buddhism. They are known as the **Triple Gem**.

Once he had given his first sermon in the deer park, the Buddha embarked upon the life of a **wandering religious teacher**. He travelled through what is now southern Nepal and eastern India. The sangha gradually expanded.

The Buddha and his followers would have lived off the **alms** provided by villagers. It would have been a harsh and dangerous existence.

At that time it was normal to travel and preach throughout the year, except during the months of the monsoon period, when the sangha lived in a monastery.

The word sangha means an assembly or community with a common goal, vision or purpose.

The Buddha embarked upon the life of a wandering religious teacher

The sangha grows

* The Buddha's father, **Suddhodana**, heard of his son's spiritual enlightenment and invited him to return to the royal palace.
* The Buddha agreed, and many members of his extended family were so impressed by his teachings that they joined the sangha.
* A cousin of the Buddha, **Ananda**, joined the sangha and became one of the Buddha's most famous disciples.
* The son of the Buddha also joined the sangha and became one of his father's principal followers.
* The Buddha also created a community of nuns.

10

The sangha allowed the Buddha's followers to practise the dharma full time, in a direct and highly disciplined way, free from the responsibilities of domestic life.

The death of the Buddha

At about the age of 80, the Buddha knew that his long life was drawing to a close.

1 He reached the village of **Kushinara**, where he was offered a meal by the village blacksmith, and shortly afterwards began to feel unwell.
2 His accompanying disciples realized that he was probably going to die.
3 The Buddha asked them if they had any final questions about his teachings. He then summarized his teachings in a final piece of advice:

'All component things decay. Strive diligently.'

> We can interpret this advice as: 'Everything in the universe is impermanent. Work hard to understand the true nature of existence.'

4 The Buddha stated that he would not appoint a successor, but would bequeath the holy dharma (the Truth) as their guide.

2 The Four Noble Truths

What are the Four Noble Truths?

When Siddhartha Gautama became the Buddha, he distilled his understanding of the nature of existence, and how to reduce or eliminate the suffering of human beings, into teachings known as the **Four Noble Truths**.

* They state the **problem** addressed by the Buddha, and also the **solution** that he proposed.
* They are not an ideology or a creed to be rigidly believed, but a practical strategy for living.

The Four Noble Truths are a practical strategy for living

This chapter explores the Four Noble Truths. These are:

1 **Suffering** is an inherent part of human existence.
2 The principal cause of suffering is **craving**. This may include craving for material possessions, or simply wishing that life could be different from the way it is.
3 If we can cease craving in all its forms, there will be an end to suffering. In order to cease craving we have to develop an objective understanding of the **nature of existence**.
4 In order to help us gain this level of understanding, the Buddha specified **a strategy** for us to follow.

The First Noble Truth

Perhaps the most obviously unsatisfactory part of life is that we know that we'll grow old, become ill and die. We try not to dwell on these **inescapable realities**, but we know they are inevitable. Growing old brings not only physical suffering, but the pain of knowing that death will separate us from those we love.

Dissatisfaction

A translation of the Buddha's teachings usually employs the word 'suffering'. However, it's sometimes easier to think of the Buddha as trying to eliminate the **unsatisfactory** nature of existence.

'...the young Gotama was stirred from the ignorance and inertia of his indulgent and overprotected life by the sight of a sick man, an old man, and a corpse.'

S. Bell

Life may seem unsatisfactory to us in many other ways. These may be relatively minor events such as heavy rain when we are out for a walk, or our favourite football team losing on Saturday afternoon.

Other **unsatisfactory aspects of life** might include:

1 having insufficient money to afford the things we want.
2 being less successful in our careers compared with others.
3 having disagreements within our family.

The key issue is **how to respond** to these situations.

● 'Life is full of unsatisfactory things!'

The Second Noble Truth

The Buddha analysed the relationship between the essentially unsatisfactory nature of life and the psychological experience of suffering.

The Buddha argued that suffering is caused not so much by the unsatisfactory event itself as by our **reaction** to it.

For most of us this is a rather different way of looking at the world:

* We normally think we are unhappy because of a certain event happening.
* We think if that event had been different or had not happened then we would be happy.

Constant craving

The Buddha argued that the ultimate cause of suffering was our **craving** for the world to be different. He argued that human beings always want things to be better, and that this was the basis of our suffering.

CASE STUDY: How craving can lead to suffering

Tom saved hard to buy a car, and knew exactly the make and model he wanted. He was pleased that he could finally afford to pay for it, and when he eventually made his purchase and drove it away he was quite happy with his new vehicle.

However, as time went by, he thought that he would really have preferred the slightly better model, and when he saw that one of his neighbours had that very model, he felt rather disappointed! He found himself craving something he knew he couldn't really afford. It seemed depressing to Tom that there was always something he wanted that was just out of his reach.

We are always craving something just out of our reach

The Third Noble Truth

According to the Buddha:

* craving is the cause of suffering
* we should remove craving from our lives
* when this happens, suffering will cease
* life will seem much more satisfactory.

We can try to exercise our **will power**, so that – in small ways at first – we are not always craving things. We may then begin to appreciate the beneficial results of the process.

It is important to remember that Buddhism is a **practical philosophy** of life as much as a religion.

The end of suffering
The removal of craving from our approach to life is the secret of becoming enlightened. However, it is easier said than done!

Self-control

We can also try to improve the **control** we have over our minds. When we achieve this:

✳ our minds will not wander, thinking about every little desire or impulse
✳ we will be more disciplined, and craving will gradually reduce.

Finally, we need to develop an insight into the **true nature of the world**. We need to recognize that new cars, nice houses and expensive holidays are superficial compared with such qualities as showing love and kindness to our fellow human beings.

Fortunately, the Buddha did not leave us to plan our own strategy to reduce craving. He gave us a **precise action plan**, which constitutes the final Noble Truth.

● The anxiety of always wanting more…

The Fourth Noble Truth

The Buddha developed a strategy to help all beings attain **release from suffering**. This is termed the **Noble Eightfold Path**. As the name suggests, it consists of eight key strategies that can be employed to attain enlightenment, or **nirvana**.

These strategies are often grouped together into three main elements, as shown in the diagram.

Although the Path is often represented as a series of stages, it can be viewed in two different ways:

1 as a **group** of strategies which can be put into practice together, and which in combination will gradually lead to enlightenment
2 as a **sequence** of strategies, which, while overlapping to some extent, can also be considered as separate stages.

The Middle Way

Before the Buddha was enlightened, he tried out a number of extreme spiritual practices, but realized that he needed strategies that were disciplined enough to help him attain nirvana, and yet not so extreme or ascetic as to damage his health. For this reason the Noble Eightfold Path is sometimes known as **'The Middle Way'**.

Buddhists would argue as follows:

* In order for this Fourth Noble Truth to help us, we need to have **confidence** in it.
* This confidence will develop as we see the **benefits** of the practice.
* We are not asked to **believe** in it, in the way that people believe in a scripture.

Buddhists are not required to believe, but to have confidence in the Buddha's teachings

3 The Noble Eightfold Path

The sections of the Path

The **Eightfold Path** consists of three major sections divided into eight subsections. The three sections involve:

1 **developing WISDOM:** trying to improve one's world view, to behave in a positive manner towards other people, and to see the world in a clearer and more objective way

2 **developing a sense of ETHICS:** speaking with truth and sensitivity, and living in a non-harmful way

3 **developing MEDITATION:** trying to control the mind, being continually mindful of our surroundings, and calming and concentrating the mind.

The Noble Eightfold Path may be summarized as follows:

* Stages 1 and 2 concern developing **Wisdom**.
* Stages 3, 4 and 5 concern developing **Ethics**.
* Stages 6, 7 and 8 concern developing **Meditation**.

This chapter explains more about the Eightfold Path.

1 CORRECT VIEW

2 CORRECT DETERMINATION

3 CORRECT SPEECH

4 CORRECT ACTION

5 CORRECT LIVELIHOOD

6 CORRECT EFFORT

7 CORRECT MINDFULNESS

8 CORRECT MEDITATION

The Buddha developed the Noble Eightfold Path to enable people to attain enlightenment, or nirvana

The Path: stages 1 and 2

Correct view

This starting point of the Buddhist pathway is to develop 'right understanding', the right way of looking at life, nature and the world. It involves:

* putting ourselves in an appropriate **frame of mind** in order to make progress on the Buddha's pathway
* having faith and **confidence** in the pathway outlined by the Buddha
* keeping an **open mind** about the teaching, so that we are prepared to learn from experience
* having **respect** for experienced Buddhist teachers so that we can learn from their advice and insights.

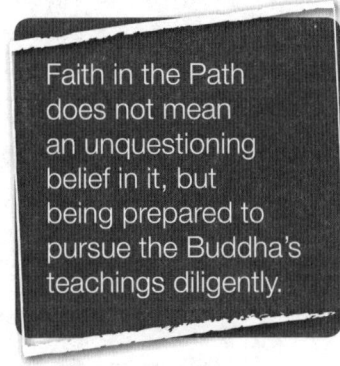

Faith in the Path does not mean an unquestioning belief in it, but being prepared to pursue the Buddha's teachings diligently.

'It is...the noble truth of the cessation of suffering and the way leading *to* the cessation of suffering, that paint a picture of how human life *ought* to be...'

A. L. Sevilla

Correct determination

This means firmly deciding to transform our lives according to the Buddha's teaching. Also known as 'correct thoughts' or 'right intention', it focuses on turning away from whatever we know to be wrong.

* At this stage on the Eightfold Path we cannot expect to have made great progress, but we need to have the **resolve to progress**.
* We need to **recognize inappropriate aspects** in our life, and firmly resolve to eliminate them.
* We need to improve the extent to which we are **friendly** and **supportive** to others.
* We need to identify occasions when we desire things, and make up our minds to **abandon these desires**.

The Path: stages 3 and 4

Correct speech

Also called 'right speech', this is the first element of the Noble Eightfold Path concerned with ethics.

* Buddhists should not **lie** or give any kind of **false impression**.
* They should not use language that is **insulting**, **rude** or likely to **hurt someone's feelings**.
* They should not use **aggressive speech** that is likely to intimidate people.
* They should not talk about others in a **mischievous** way when they are not present.
* They should not talk about people in such a way as to **undermine their position**.

'And what is right speech? Abstaining from lying, from divisive speech, from abusive speech, and from idle chatter: This is called right speech.'

Pali Canon

Correct action

Also called 'right action' or 'right conduct', this is the second element of the Path concerned with ethics.

* Buddhists should behave in a way that is **appropriate to the spiritual life**.
* They should not **attack, harm** or **kill other living things**.
* They should not **steal** from the belongings of others.
* They should not be **over-indulgent** in the pleasures of the senses. This includes not being excessive in eating and drinking, as well as not participating excessively in sensual or sexual activities.

● 'I will not have that extra piece of cake.'

The Path: stages 5 and 6

Correct livelihood

This is also concerned with ethics. Buddhists should take care that the type of **job** or **career** they take up will not harm other living beings.

* They should not have a job that financially, or in any other way, **exploits people**.
* They should not have a job concerned with **killing living things**. This might include raising animals for slaughter, being a butcher, or hunting and fishing.

* It would be difficult for Buddhists to be members of the **armed forces** unless they felt there was a greater moral obligation forcing them to take part.
* They should not be involved in the use or selling of **drugs**, including alcohol and tobacco.

> A Buddhist livelihood **should not harm others.**

Correct effort

At this stage of the Eightfold Path, Buddhists recognize that the mind has to be controlled through persistent effort if progress towards enlightenment is to be made.

* Ideas and thoughts come and go and disturb the **calmness** of the mind. Some of these ideas and thoughts may be positive, while others may be negative.
* Ideas should not be forced from the mind, but the undesirable ones should be gradually **eased away** and replaced by calmness and positive thoughts.
* **Continuous effort** is required to achieve this. If we do not sustain the effort, undesirable thoughts will enter the mind.

A Buddhist tries to ease away negative thoughts, leaving their brain calm and purely positive

The Path: stages 7 and 8

Correct mindfulness

In order to help control the mind, Buddhists practise **mindfulness**. This means focusing all our attention on the **present moment**, and the things we are doing right now. We can focus on:

✳ the coming and going of our **thoughts**
✳ our **body** and the way it is moving and feeling
✳ the way our **feelings** arise and then change.

If they continue to be mindful, Buddhists argue that their minds gradually become more **stable**.

Learning to **understand the mind** is at the heart of Buddhism. Mindfulness – concentrating the mind on the thing we are doing in the present moment – helps train the mind to remain calm, so that it is then able to analyse the world and bring insight into the nature of existence.

Correct meditation

The final stage of the Noble Eightfold Path is that of meditation practice:

* This consists of a range of **mental disciplines** designed to train the mind.
* Normally our minds are easily distracted and move quickly from one thought to another.
* Meditation trains our minds to be **calmer** and more **consistent**.
* Our minds are then in a position to reflect on the **characteristics of the world,** such as the impermanence of things and the nature of human existence.

● 'In Buddhism meditation enables us to control and pacify the mind.'

4 The conquest of suffering

The Buddhist view of suffering

The purpose of the Buddha's teachings is to enable people to understand the causes of suffering and the true nature of reality, so that they have an **honest** and **objective view of the world**. With this view, the suffering that is an inevitable part of life may be reduced or even eliminated.

Suffering might be either **physical**, as in illness, or **psychological**, as in stress. By understanding the causes of the troubles and anxieties of life, we may become less affected by them.

By reducing our suffering we attain a calmer, more balanced view of life

The Buddhist word for 'suffering' is **dukkha**, which comes from the old Indian language known as Pali, in which many of the early Buddhist scriptures were written. Dukkha is normally translated as 'suffering', but it really means 'the things in life we would prefer to be different'.

Examples of dukkha include:

* the **sadness** we feel when a loved one dies
* the **anxiety** we experience when our children are ill
* the **uncertainties** we feel about our own future
* the **stress** we feel at work
* the **pain** we feel when we are ill.

This chapter explores suffering in more detail.

Why do we suffer?

For Buddhists, the world will never be a perfect place:

* There will always be sad and unhappy events.
* Many of these events may be completely outside our control.
* Our loved ones may become seriously ill or natural disasters may overcome us.

The Buddhist analysis of this situation is that we may not be able to change the **events** themselves, but what we can do is change our **attitudes** to them:

1 We can learn to appreciate that unsatisfactory events are a natural part of life.
2 We can try to develop a more relaxed attitude to them.

'We cannot prevent problems from arising. That is simply the nature of life.'

G. Farrer-Halls

Buddhism goes to the core of every individual human being's concern – suffering and how to avoid it. The table below shows some of the key ideas Buddhism offers about suffering.

1 Our attitude	According to Buddhists, suffering arises in **our attitude** to a situation, not to the situation itself.
2 Not a magic solution	Buddhism is **not a magic solution** to the pain caused by the death of a loved one or by serious illness.
3 Positive way	Buddhism can help us to face situations in a more **positive way**.
4 Not negative	Buddhism is **not negative,** even though it analyses unhappy events and suffering.
5 Well adjusted	Buddhism is trying to help us lead more positive, **well-adjusted** lives.

Freedom from suffering

It may be thought that Buddhism is a rather selfish religion, in that it seems preoccupied with suffering, which may seem to encourage people to think only of their own suffering.

However, if we are preoccupied with our own pain and unhappiness, we cannot be of much help to others. By helping to free us of too much concern for our own suffering, Buddhism liberates us to help others.

Free from concern for our own suffering, we are more able to help others

This approach helps reduce our **egoism** – our preoccupation with the 'self'. In fact, one of the main teachings of Buddhism is that there is no real self, and that we should continually try to eliminate our concerns about the person we think we are.

* We can develop **empathy** with the suffering of others. The main strategy used by Buddhists to achieve this is meditation.
* This helps to calm the mind, and to enable us to see the world clearly and objectively.

Empathy and compassion
These are key Buddhist virtues, or desirable characteristics. A Buddhist aims to recognize that all other people – and indeed all living things – aspire to happiness, and that putting yourself in others' shoes can help us to know how best to help them.

● Buddhism encourages us to think less of our own needs, and more of those of others

Not an act of faith

Buddhism is not an **act of faith**.

It is a **practical strategy** to use in everyday life.

In order to give us a fresh perspective on life, we have to use this strategy **regularly** and with determination.

Buddhism is *not* something to believe in; it is something to practise **every moment of our lives**.

Buddhists will sometimes say to each other in conversation 'How is your practice going?' It is a way of recognizing that the mind has to be continually trained in order to enable the person to reach enlightenment. The person may reply: 'Well, I have been tending to worry about trivial things recently, so I am increasing the number of meditation sessions slightly.'

44

What are the results of Buddhist practice?

Following the principles of Buddhism may not lead everyone to nirvana, or enlightenment, but it should help to **reduce the suffering** we feel, even though the actual source of the suffering will remain. However, suffering will not be diminished unless we make the effort to practise Buddhist principles regularly and **conscientiously**.

Top tip
Remember, individual people will benefit to a different extent from Buddhist practice. Even a slight reduction in suffering is valuable.

● Like juggling, Buddhism needs practice…and plenty of it!

Buddhism and ethics

Buddhism helps us to keep personal suffering **in context**, and to learn compassion and loving kindness towards other people. By helping us to act in a more moral way we can be of more help to others. Buddhism helps us to:

☐ **empathize** with the feelings of others
☐ **treat others** as we would like them to treat us
☐ **help others** whenever possible
☐ **interpret events** in a balanced way
☐ **calm our mind** as much as possible.

All these actions should help to reduce our suffering.

'Pay no attention to the faults of others, things done or left undone by others. Consider only what by oneself is done or left undone.'

Buddhist proverb

46

CASE STUDY: Reducing suffering through meditation

Jane worked in a high-pressure job. She had continual targets to meet. Many of her colleagues were in the same position, and this created tensions between them. A restructuring of her organization was also being planned, and this caused her to worry about her job security.

She started to attend Buddhist meditation classes. As a result, Jane found that she felt slightly calmer at work, which helped her to establish better relationships with colleagues. In the restructuring she was given a slightly lower-status job, but this did not bother her too much. After several weeks, she decided to apply for jobs elsewhere, and managed to get one at her previous level.

5 The concept of impermanence

Impermanence and change

The concept of impermanence starts with the observation that both living and non-living things **change with time**. This is perhaps most obvious with living organisms.

The Buddha argued that everything in the universe was in a state of constant change, or impermanence. Impermanence is one of the key concepts of Buddhism, and one of the so-called **Three Marks of Existence**. These are:

1 **impermanence** (anicca in Pali, the scriptural language of Theravada Buddhism)
2 **suffering** (dukkha in Pali)
3 **no-self** (anatta in Pali).

Impermanence is evident in the following phenomena:

* **Human beings** grow, change appearance and shape, and eventually become ill and die.
* Our bodies are in a continual state of change.
* **Rocks** and **mountains** are subject to erosion by water and wind.
* The water in **lakes** and **seas** evaporates, only to return as rain.
* The carbon dioxide we breathe out is converted by **plants** into carbohydrates.
* The **universe** is in a continual process of cyclical change.

This chapter explores some of the ideas of impermanence in more detail.

Impermanence is one of Buddhism's Three Marks of Existence
....

Aggregation and disaggregation

All change

Aggregation and disaggregation are an **inevitable** part of life:

* When living things disaggregate and decay, the molecules of which they are formed separate.
* Those same molecules eventually aggregate and come together in different ways to form new life.
* Ultimately, that life will end and decay, and the cycle will repeat itself.
* In the universe, change, transition and impermanence are the norm.

> It is said in Buddhism that there is no self because there is impermanence, and because there is impermanence, there is suffering.

● All living things grow, change and die

52

Human mutability

The nature of change as a cyclical process also operates within the **physiological** processes of human beings:

* We know that our hearts contract to pump out blood, and then expand. Then they contract again.
* We breathe in and then breathe out; then we breathe in again.
* The cells of our body are getting older and some are dying all the time.
* Our bodies are never the same from one minute to the next.
* The Buddha taught that change and transition are part of the nature of things.

'If you are beside yourself with joy, tears are not far behind.'

Tibetan saying

Psychological impermanence

Not only does impermanence operate at a physical level, among plants, animals and the inanimate world, but it also operates at a **psychological level**. Contemplating and grasping the real nature of impermanence are at the core of Buddhism.

1 If we observe our mind we notice it is in a continual state of flux.
2 The mind is rarely still.
3 Ideas come into the mind, stay for a while and then slip away.
4 Sometimes unpleasant ideas enter the mind and stay for a long time, causing us distress.
5 If we are patient, however, they eventually diminish.

Learning how to **cope** with our changing minds is one of the central elements of Buddhism. The Buddha taught us ways of controlling the mind so that we would be less affected by the coming and going of ideas.

It is one thing to understand impermanence logically, but quite another to **truly understand** it.

* When we look at our bodies it is difficult to imagine them as merely a collection of bones when we are dead.
* Although we know logically this is what will happen, it is difficult to imagine because we have never seen it before.
* Therefore it is difficult to learn from the nature of impermanence.

Buddhist monks and nuns sometimes meditate by looking at a real human skeleton in order to try to understand the real nature of impermanence.

Contemplating and grasping the real nature of impermanence are at the core of Buddhism

Non-attachment

* It is essential to cultivate non-attachment if we are to live a serene and happy life in a world of constant change.
* Non-attachment helps us take a **balanced** view of things.

* If we understand that things are impermanent, we will treat them with less importance.
* The Buddha taught us to be non-attached to **material objects** as well as to **pleasures** or **sensations**.

'Buddhism does value non-attachment towards material goods, and promotes the virtue of having fewer wants...'

D. R. Loy

It is easy, for example, to become over-attached to the pleasures of eating. The Buddha would have advised us to eat simple, wholesome food **in moderation**, enough for sustaining health.

Material things

Once we look at material objects and realize that they are all eventually going to decay, it changes our **perception** of them to some extent. Perhaps they don't seem quite as important as they did previously.

For example, when we have work done on our house, we can be very fussy about it. We treat a new carpet or kitchen very carefully, and worry in case the slightest stain should appear or some damage is done.

Non-attachment teaches us to take a more balanced, 'philosophical' view of life.

● Keeping things perfect is impossible and can drive us crazy if we attach too much importance to them…

Learning to let go

When we have begun to understand the significance of impermanence, we can learn to **let go** of problems and anxieties, knowing that they will to some extent resolve themselves. This is typical of a Buddhist approach to life.

* Learning to let go of things is another way of thinking about **non-attachment**.
* It's not the same as **ignoring** a problem or **not caring** about it.
* It is, however, **accepting** that problems will sometimes follow their own course.
* When we allow them to do this, sometimes a **solution** develops naturally.

Top tip
If you can't fall asleep at night because of something on your mind, practise letting go through meditation.

Non-attachment = release from desire or craving = release from suffering

Here's a summary of the Buddhist attitude to life:

Understanding impermanence is partly to appreciate that life follows its own **rhythm** of change.

By practising **non-attachment** we permit life to develop naturally.

This can help us to be more **relaxed** and **at ease** with ourselves.

It can **reduce suffering**.

The Buddha said:
'We forget that our lives are transitory, and we quarrel with each other as if we are going to live for ever. But, if we face the fact of death, our quarrels will come to an end.'

6 The purpose of meditation

Approaches to meditation

Buddhist **meditation** involves achieving control of the mind in order to achieve enlightenment. The strategies used in meditation vary somewhat between different schools of Buddhism.

The Buddha taught two broad approaches to meditation. These are:

1 meditation to calm the mind
2 meditation to gain insight.

Meditation is an essential part of Buddhist practice and needs to be practised **regularly** and **diligently** in order to make spiritual progress.

Meditation is an essential part of Buddhist practice

This chapter explores the Buddhist concept of meditation and the different kinds of meditation practice.

* In order to calm the mind, the Buddhist develops **concentration**. The mind is trained to focus on just one thing.
* The usual object selected is the steady inhalation and exhalation of the **breath**.
* When the mind is calm it is easier to develop **insight**.

The Buddhist starts to gain insights into the true nature of the world. These insights are analysed in terms of:

* impermanence * suffering * no-self.

Ultimately the Buddhist gains a clear understanding of reality – such that all suffering is reduced or eliminated – and obtains **enlightenment**.

First steps to meditation

You can practise meditation in a variety of locations and postures:

✳ It is usually best to find a **peaceful location** away from noise or potential disturbance.

✳ The traditional posture for meditation is the **lotus posture**, which entails:

 » sitting upright – usually on a cushion or low stool – with legs crossed and each foot resting on the opposite thigh.

 » slightly inclining the head forwards and resting the hands on the knees or in the lap.

> The lotus is a difficult posture for those unaccustomed to it, and should only be attempted after gradual practice.

● The lotus position

Meditators can use **other postures**, such as kneeling or sitting.

Breath awareness meditation

The first type of meditation is termed, in Pali, **Anapanasati**. This translates as 'being mindful of the breathing'.

1 In order to develop calmness, the Buddhist needs an object on which to concentrate. The Buddha recommended concentrating on the breath.
2 The meditator focuses on the way in which the breath enters the nostrils, and then leaves the nostrils.
3 There is inhalation and exhalation.
4 At first the mind will wander away from the breath to other subjects.
5 However, the meditator gradually and gently brings the mind back to concentrate on the breath.

'With increasing concentration the mind becomes more tranquil, and its activity diminishes.'

C. Erricker

Insight meditation

When the mind is relatively calm it becomes easier to develop insight.

Insight meditation, or **Vipassana** in Pali, aims to help the Buddhist achieve insight into the nature of reality. It includes any meditation technique that cultivates insight through contemplation, introspection, observation of bodily sensations, analytic meditation and observations about lived experience.

It helps the meditator analyse phenomena or objects, and to see them as a reflection of impermanence, suffering and no-self.

* As thoughts come into the mind, the meditator appreciates that they are impermanent, and that there is no permanent self to be harmed.
* This understanding helps to reduce suffering.
* The ultimate result of such insights is a state of enlightenment.

Some Buddhists argue that **Vipassana** should not be seen as always following **Anapanasati**.

In reality, a calm mind helps to produce insight, and insight helps to induce calmness:

Calm ↔ Insight

In other words the two are mutually supportive.

A related concept in Buddhism is **mindfulness**. When meditators watch the breath, they are being mindful of it. Mindfulness can be used in everyday life as a form of meditation. When we are doing something such as house repairs or shopping, our minds often wander away to other things.

'Do not dwell in the past, do not dream of the future, concentrate the mind on the present moment.'

Siddhartha Gautama

Mindfulness

We can be doing one thing and yet our minds may be worrying about something else. This does not contribute towards our **peace of mind**, but encourages suffering. A more Buddhist approach to life is to keep gently returning our minds to the thing we are doing. This is the practice of **mindfulness**.

If we practice mindfulnesss diligently it helps prevent extraneous thoughts clouding our minds and potentially causing suffering.

● Whatever we do, whether it's the washing up or parachuting, we need to keep our minds on what we are doing...

Walking meditation

Walking meditation is an alternative form of meditation for calming the mind. It combines **slow**, **steady** and **controlled movement** with a mindful approach to the act of walking, as follows:

1 Mark out the beginning and end of a short path for the meditation.
2 Walk slowly in measured steps from one end to the other, and then return the same way.
3 Repeat the process a number of times.
4 During the meditation, try to be mindful of your feet touching the ground – first one, then the other.
5 Be aware of your bodily movements and sensations as you walk.
6 Also be mindful of the number of strides you need to cover the path.

'Meditation brings wisdom; lack of meditation leaves ignorance.'
Siddhartha Gautama

Zen meditation

The Japanese form of Buddhism, known as **Zen**, has distinctive features associated with its meditation practice. Zen sitting meditation is known as **zazen**. There are two main kinds of zazen:

1 In the **Soto Zen** school of Buddhism, meditators calmly watch ideas enter the mind, and subsequently leave the mind.
2 In the **Rinzai Zen** school, meditators reflect upon a koan.

The koan

A koan is a puzzling or **enigmatic saying** given to the Zen meditator, usually by the abbot of a monastery. The meditator must reflect on the koan and attempt to find a solution. The koan often appears to defy logic.

Its purpose is to encourage the meditator to think more spontaneously and to abandon a purely rational solution.

70

Zen meditation often lasts for sustained periods and is accompanied by periods of repetitive physical work. In a monastery the daily routine may require monks to meditate for several hours a day, interspersed with short breaks and periods of work performed with the same mindfulness.

This is intended to provide a time for both the practice of **mindfulness** and for **reflection** upon the **koan**.

The paradox of Buddhist meditation is that the practitioner aspires to enlightenment, and yet must simultaneously not be attached to this end. Buddhist meditation thus demands a regular disciplined practice combined with a natural spontaneity of approach.

Zen meditation takes place over long periods

7 The doctrine of no-self

Understanding no-self

According to Buddhism, no-self is one of the three characteristics of existence, along with impermanence and suffering. The doctrine of **no-self** (or **anatta**, in Pali) derives partly from the concept of **impermanence**. The human body is considered to be impermanent, in that eventually it will disaggregate and decay; the elements of which it is made will separate.

No-self is the teaching that there is **no permanent soul** or ego, or 'I' or 'me', in the human body.

No-self is the teaching that there is no permanent soul or ego

Since we are constantly changing beings, and not permanent, fixed entities, Buddhists find it very difficult to imagine the body having a permanent soul. They wonder where the soul would come from initially and imagine peering inside the body looking for the location of the soul:

* Where would it be?
* What would it look like?
* Where would it go after death?

Questions such as these perhaps tend to persuade Buddhists that there is no soul or self, simply because there is **no scientific** or **empirical evidence** for one.

This chapter explores the implications of this conclusion.

What is the self?

The Buddha's teaching of no-self is about letting go of our egos so that we can become open to the present moment. If we always think about the world from the point of view of a 'self', then this will almost inevitably lead to suffering. For example:

* If we reflect upon our material possessions and think how intelligent we are to have acquired them, then we are becoming very attached to them.
* If we were then to lose them for any reason we would be very unhappy and would suffer.

However, there are other ways of thinking about the idea of self and no-self.

● 'Someone took my laptop!'

Very often, we become **attached** to things, not just because we intrinsically like them, but because we think that they reflect well on us.

* People like to have a smart sports car because it is a reflection of their **social status**. It is an extension of their ego.
* People like to talk about their expensive holidays because they feel they imply something complimentary about their 'self'.
* They like to wear designer label clothes because they reflect well upon their **self-image**.

If they could not 'express' themselves in that way, then they would be unhappy.

> ## '...a sincere practising Buddhist could not interact harmoniously and continuously in the consumerist society.'
> T. Lorentz

Our sense of self

* If people are unkind to us, our 'feelings' are hurt. We feel that our 'self' has been hurt or **damaged**.
* If people say spiteful or insulting things to us, we feel hurt. We feel as if our sense of self has been **undermined**.

78

> **Top tip**
> If we suddenly lose our wealth and have to manage on very little, our sense of self is hurt because it is no longer propped up by our acquisitions.

● Our sense of self is easily undermined and we suffer because of it

If, however, we do not think in terms of a 'self', we won't feel hurt if we lose our possessions or if we are insulted. We will not suffer, and will be in a state of **equanimity**.

* It can be said that the doctrine of no-self is not a doctrinal teaching to be learned and accepted as truth.
* Rather it is a way of **perceiving ourselves**, which we learn from experience.
* If we consider the trials and tribulations of life, and consider them from the point of view of someone who does not possess a self, we realize that they do not affect us.
* We remain **immune** from them in a way that supports the teaching of no-self.

'Peace comes from within. Do not seek it without.'
Siddhartha Gautama

The concept of anatta

One of the basic issues of the idea of no-self (anatta) is whether the concept is intended to be **analytic** and **philosophical**, or whether it is intended to be **empirical**:

* If the former, then we would seek to resolve it by philosophical discussion and analysis.
* If, on the other hand, it is intended to be an empirical concept, then we would seek evidence in our observations of human beings.

Buddhists, however, generally do not tend to treat anatta as an intellectual idea, to be proved by logic or reasoning. It is more often treated as a practical, empirical idea whose consequences we can observe in everyday life.

Anatta seems to minimize the extent of suffering

The advantages of anatta

As I have already argued, Buddhists believe there to be **practical advantages** in accepting the idea of no-self. If we accept the assumption, then it seems to minimize the extent of suffering.

Buddhists would suggest that:

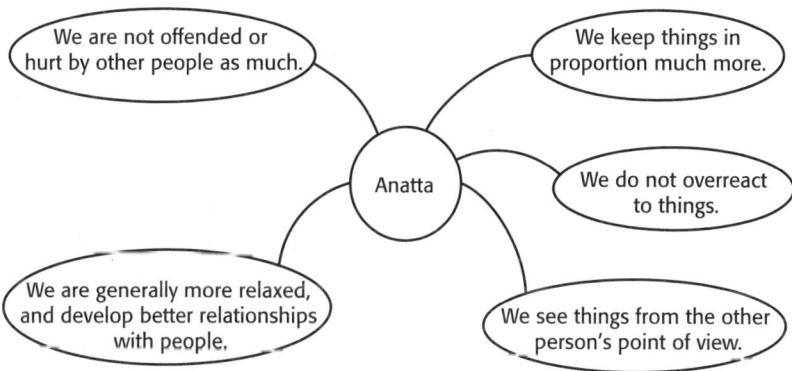

We are not offended or hurt by other people as much.

We keep things in proportion much more.

Anatta

We do not overreact to things.

We are generally more relaxed, and develop better relationships with people.

We see things from the other person's point of view.

No-self and happiness

Through the process of meditation Buddhists begin to appreciate that **nothing** in the universe has an independent and permanent existence. Everything comes and goes.

Many of us would probably like to think that there was something permanent in us that we could think of as our 'self', but Buddhists consider this to be an **unhelpful** idea.

It is counter-productive to leading **a happy life.**

Everything comes
and goes
. . . .

> The human 'self' to which we are so attached is, according to Buddhists, impermanent like everything else. From one point of view, we would perhaps like to believe in the self, but the idea only seems to lead to unhappiness.

To summarize:

1 Buddhism teaches that the self and any associated ideas are **impermanent**.
2 If an idea about an independent self comes into the mind, it stays for a while and then disperses.
3 Buddhists argue that all things eventually **disperse**, whether they are material objects, ideas or thoughts.
4 Once we understand that the coming together of things in the universe is not the norm, and that there is an inevitable tendency for things to separate and disaggregate, we are more **accepting of life**.
5 We do not cling to things as much, for we know that ultimately we will be separated from them.

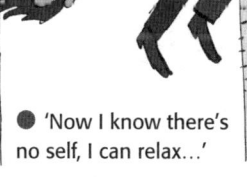

● 'Now I know there's no self, I can relax…'

8 Achieving nirvana

What is nirvana?

Nirvana (or **nibbana**, in Pali) is the state in which all desire and longing has been removed from the human spirit. The term means 'blowing out' or 'extinguishing', and signifies the extinguishing of all desires, attachments and longing, and also the extinguishing of a distorted view of life.

The person who has achieved nirvana sees the world **as it really is**, in a balanced and objective way.

The person who has achieved nirvana sees the world as it really is

People who have attained nirvana:

* do not wish for **material possessions**
* do not wish for the world to be different from the way it is
* have removed all traces of **delusion** from the way they perceive the world
* accept the apparently undesirable elements of life, such as illness, old age and death, simply because they are **an inevitable part** of the cycle of life.

This does not mean, however, that Buddhists are completely passive, and would not like to change the poverty and inequalities in the world.

This chapter explores the concept of nirvana and how it might be reached.

Beliefs about nirvana

* Buddhists who have attained nirvana do what they can to be **kind and generous** to people, while accepting that some aspects of the human condition **cannot be altered**.
* Buddhists believe that nirvana can be achieved **in this life**. It is therefore not comparable with concepts of heaven, or of an eternal kingdom attained after death.
* Nirvana is, Buddhists believe, a **real psychological state** achievable during our present lifetime.

88

> It is important not to think of nirvana as a state Buddhists are striving to achieve. Rather nirvana is the result of **not striving**, of not being attached to the gaining of possessions or the achieving of things.

* The concept of 'striving' towards a goal is **antithetical** to Buddhism.
* The person in a state of nirvana is not susceptible to **inappropriate reactions**.
* If someone is angry with the person in a state of nirvana, that person will **not overreact**, or display irritation and anger.
* The person who has achieved nirvana can **control** his or her emotions, and will remain calm even under conditions of great stress.

● Keep calm!

Freedom from desire

Those who have attained nirvana don't discriminate between that which is **desirable** and that which is **undesirable**:

1 If they see attractive delicious food on one table, and plain, less enticing food on another, they don't display a preference for one rather than the other.
2 They don't try to eat the pleasant food, and avoid the plain food.
3 They don't try to eat the plain food, and avoid the pleasant food.
4 An enlightened person is content with whatever food is offered.
5 When people can do this, they are inherently free.

For most human beings, life is a continual effort to **seek out the 'best'** – the most attractive, the most desirable, and in contemporary times, something with a 'designer label.'

The continual search for desirable things is a trap

The trap of desire

The continual search for the most desirable things in life is, according to Buddhist thought, a **trap** that destroys our freedom, and ultimately makes us unhappy.

* True freedom lies in avoiding this trap.
* The Buddhist is happy with whatever he or she receives or is given.

The true nature of nirvana

In some ways it is a mistake for Buddhists to think that they are gradually moving *towards* nirvana, since it does not exist as something towards which people can move. In fact, nirvana is achieved by **letting go** of any idea of moving towards something.

Nirvana is described by some as being **calm**, in the sense of not reacting violently to events, and behaving in a restrained and balanced way.

Is nirvana a place?

* Nirvana is sometimes imagined to be a place like heaven: somewhere we go to after death, as long as we have led a virtuous life.

* In fact, according to Buddhists, we can achieve nirvana **in this life**, since it is concerned with the way in which we react skilfully to the world around us.

* Some argue that nirvana is **indefinable**, since it is not a concept we can define in a linguistic or an analytic sense. Rather, it is a state or condition that must be experienced.

> Nirvana is sometimes described as a state of bliss or extreme happiness. It is not, however, the type of happiness associated with winning the lottery. It is a happiness of great peace and tranquillity.

The person who has attained nirvana has, in a sense, achieved all of the **finest, most noble qualities** associated with human beings.

* Such people demonstrate great **compassion** towards others.
* They realize that *all* human beings suffer – some more than others and in different ways – since existence *is* suffering.
* This tendency to suffer provides a **link** between all human beings.

Top tip
Those who are enlightened are able to have a profound sense of **empathy** with the suffering of others.

● A link between all human beings...

The attainment of nirvana

☐ For Buddhists the condition of nirvana is not something that is part of a **person's destiny.**

☐ Some people may be more i**nclined** than others to a Buddhist perception of the world.

☐ Such people might be predisposed to making more **spiritual progress**, while others persist in clinging to material possessions and rigid views of the world.

☐ Generally, however, the attainment of nirvana depends upon the **hard work** and **diligence** of the aspirant. It does not depend upon the intervention of a deity or other spiritual power.

☐ The more effort that is exerted in terms of meditation and the other elements of the **Noble Eightfold Path**, the more likely the person is to attain enlightenment.

'Seeing the conditioned nature of things, the enlightened mind is not enslaved by them.'

Kulananda

CASE STUDY: The enlightened mind

The mind of the person who has attained nirvana does not respond to events that are part of the cycle of existence. When parts of their body begin to show signs of ageing, and they look less attractive than before, the enlightened person simply regards this as part of an **inevitable process**. They do not feel upset or disheartened by it.

When they become ill, and can no longer do their usual physical activities, they do not feel discouraged. They accept this as a normal feature of getting older and as part of the normal pattern of existence, and of passing on to a new existence. Even the prospect of **death** is accepted with equanimity.

9 Theravada Buddhism

The teaching of the Elders

In the centuries after the death of the Buddha, his teachings began to spread. In the third century BCE, the emperor **Ashoka** encouraged missionaries to spread Buddhist teachings, and the **Theravada** school of Buddhism became established in Sri Lanka, Burma, Thailand and other countries in South-East Asia.

The written Buddhist teachings are known as the **Pali Canon**. Some people think Theravada is the school of Buddhism closest to the Buddha's original teachings.

The name Theravada means 'The teaching of the Elders'.

Theravada is one of the two major schools of Buddhism

This chapter describes how the teachings of the Buddha spread.

* After the Buddha's death, his teachings were **memorized by monks**, and repeated over and over again in chanting. In this way the teachings were passed from generation to generation.
* During the first century BCE, the teachings were **written down in Pali**, during the Fourth Buddhist Council. These teachings are known as the **Pali Canon**.
* The Pali Canon exists in three different sections called **pitaka**, or baskets.
* One of the pitaka, the **Vinayha Pitaka**, includes the code of conduct for monks, while the other pitaka contain records and analyses of Buddhist teachings.

The Theravada monastery

In the Theravada tradition, monks and nuns lead a very **disciplined, ordered life**:

* They rise early, usually before dawn, and gather in the monastery for communal meditation and chanting in Pali.
* There may be a simple breakfast.
* During the early morning they go on the alms round, during which laypeople have the opportunity to support the sangha, or community of monks and nuns, by providing gifts of food.

The sangha has a very important teaching role in Buddhism.

'...it is the task of the community to preserve and hand over the teaching of the Buddha (the dhamma) to following generations.'

O. Freiberger

* Before noon, the monks and nuns eat the only proper meal of the day.
* Most of the day is spent either in **meditation**, doing **chores** around the monastery or **teaching**.
* Sometimes the head of the monastery gives a talk in the evening.
* The monks and nuns are allowed to have only the barest essentials needed to sustain life.
* They are not permitted to handle money.

● The alms bowl is a symbol of the Buddha's teachings on non-attachment

Theravada traditions

Monks and nuns are required to be careful about what they accept as **alms**, and how they accept it:

* They would not be able to accept a financial donation to the monastery, if it was placed in the alms bowl.
* In addition, a monk or nun would not normally accept anything with their hands from someone of the opposite gender. It would have to be placed into the alms bowl.

Monks and nuns may **bless people** (for example at a marriage ceremony), but could not officiate at the marriage.

> The role of Buddhist monks and nuns is essentially to practise and study Buddhism and, when they are sufficiently experienced, to teach the **dhamma** to others.

The Theravada tradition has tended to distinguish between ordained **monks and nuns** on the one hand, and **laypeople** on the other, in terms of their involvement in Buddhism:

* **Monks and nuns** first and foremost preserve the doctrine and discipline of Buddhism.
* The religious practice of ordained people is more demanding, and they are expected to provide a living example for the laypeople.
* There is an assumption that they are more likely to attain nirvana.
* **Laypeople** may involve themselves in administrative roles in a temple or monastery.
* They may also help maintain the infrastructure of the temple.
* Laypeople help to provide the noonday meal for the monks and nuns.

> Boys from seven years of age may be ordained as novice monks, although the more usual age is 20.

Monastic dress

When Theravada monks and nuns are ordained, they leave their life in normal society and assume the life of a wandering mendicant who has no home. They:

1 **shave their heads** as a sign of becoming a mendicant
2 wear the characteristic simple **orange** or **ochre robe**
3 may use their robe as a blanket, groundsheet, head-cover or windbreak.

Monks and nuns assume the life of a wandering mendicant

In the time of the Buddha it seems likely that the first monks wore their hair long, like present-day Hindu **sadhus**. The Buddha, however, recommended shaving the head and beard. Traditionally, monks dye their own cloth, and then cut and sew the material, in order to make a robe.

Monastic possessions

The only possessions a monk can have are:

* three ochre robes
* an alms bowl
* a razor
* a drinking water filter
* a needle and thread
* a waistband to hold the robes together.

The purpose is that monks and nuns should lead a **simple, non-acquisitive life** that supports the discipline of their practice.

A monk's or nun's home

The residence of a monk or nun was meant to be very basic. It should simply provide shelter from the wind, rain and hot sun. It should not provide anything to distract the monk or nun from their responsibilities.

Rich lay devotees built the monasteries, as it was considered an act of merit not only to feed but also to shelter the monks.

Theravada conduct

* Monks and nuns are expected to be careful in the company of laypeople of the opposite sex, and to avoid behaviour that might be construed as **improper**.
* The relationship between monks, nuns and laypeople is a **symbiotic** one. Laypeople help to provide the necessities of life for the monks and nuns, while the latter provide dhamma teachings.

The Buddha advised his monks to be careful not to harm other living things, whether plant or animal. This has resulted in a strong tradition of non-violence.

'If you do not know the laws of right conduct, you **cannot** form your character.'
Swami Sivananda

* Much of the conduct expected of a Theravada monk or nun is a reflection of mindfulness.
* They are expected to observe, **carefully and continually**, the way they move, speak, think and act, in order to be sensitive and careful to their surroundings.
* Monks and nuns traditionally **travel for most of the year**, except during the monsoon rains, which in South-East Asia normally arrive between July and October. During this period the monks often remain resident in one particular place because it is difficult to travel. This is when they take part in an annual meditation retreat.

When a monk or nun has been ordained for ten such retreats, he or she is usually assumed to have sufficient knowledge and wisdom to teach the **dhamma**.

10 Mahayana Buddhism

The Great Vehicle

Apart from Theravada Buddhism, the **Mahayana** is the other main school of Buddhism. It is found largely in Nepal, Tibet, China, Japan and Bhutan. The term Mahayana, which means the **'Great Vehicle'**, probably evolved around the first century BCE, and can be identified in the writings of the **Lotus Sutra**.

The Mahayana emphasizes the role of the 'bodhisattva'. This is a person who does not concentrate on his or her own liberation, but strives primarily to help others achieve that goal.

Mahayana Buddhism is very **varied**, partly because it has been influenced to some extent by the specific cultures of the countries in which it has developed. Nevertheless. it retains its devotion to the central teachings and precepts of the historical Buddha:

* There is a strong tradition of the importance of religious practice in **monasteries**.
* Mahayana monks and nuns adhere to the same **code of conduct** as other Buddhist monasteries.
* The study of Buddhist scriptures, or **sutras**, is a characteristic element of the Mahayana.

This chapter explores the Mahayana tradition in more detail.

Mahayana is the other main school of Buddhism

The Mahayana tradition

The Mahayana tradition is very eclectic:

* It puts great emphasis on strict **meditational practice**.
* It has a much greater involvement with **devotion** than is typical in the Theravada tradition.
* There is also an assumption among devotees of the Mahayana that one can gain **esoteric spiritual advantages** from Mahayana practice.
* The Buddha is not simply perceived as the historical Buddha, but as a **mystical reality** able to help those who devote themselves to him.
* The **bodhisattva** represents the ideal values of truth and wisdom, and of generosity towards one's fellow human beings.
* It is heavily influenced by local religious and cultural ideas.

'In the practice of tolerance, one's enemy is the best teacher.'
The Dalai Lama

The bodhisattva

The bodhisattva pursues his or her own path to eliminate suffering and gain nirvana. The **ultimate purpose**, however, is not ego-centred, but focused on helping all other beings achieve enlightenment.

The bodhisattva thus comes to represent a sense of universal moral and spiritual values.

● The bodhisattva is motivated by compassion for all living things

Buddha nature

A concept found widely in the Mahayana approach is that of the **Buddha nature**. This idea assumes that all beings possess the essential spirit of the Buddha within themselves.

This is not the same, however, as saying that there is a soul within all of us. That would contradict the philosophy of **no-self**, or the idea that there is no specific soul to pass on when we die.

The idea of the Buddha nature is that there is a **potential for enlightenment** within all of us. This potential emphasizes the nature of emptiness, or the potential to be non-attached to the material world.

● 'I've found my Buddha nature!'

114

The Buddha nature within us can act as a **motivator** to encourage us to seek a higher spirituality. It motivates us to seek an enlightened view of the world, and to try to find a solution to the problem of suffering.

Buddha as God?

A major difference from the Theravada is that within the Mahayana, the Buddha figure has almost evolved into a deity that can be worshipped, and in whom devotees can have faith. Such faith in the **divine Buddha** is regarded as an aid in achieving enlightenment.

The Buddha is perceived as transcending earthly life, and existing in a heavenly state. From this state he is able to assist people, as they progress through a cycle of rebirths, to gradually achieve enlightenment.

Vajrayana and Pure Land Buddhism

Vajrayana

Vajrayana is a branch of Mahayana Buddhism, often known as **Tantric Buddhism**. Knowledge of the Vajrayana is passed from the teacher to the student in a line of succession. This school has a strong emphasis on:

1 the use of religious **ritual**
2 the significance of **iconography**
3 the **mantra**, or holy utterance.

The ultimate purpose of a Vajrayana devotee is to gain **Buddhahood** and enlightenment.

> Vajrayana teachings are sometimes described as **esoteric**, in that they are acquired through direct guru-to-pupil transmission.

Vajrayana has a strong emphasis on the mantra

Pure Land

✣ Pure Land Buddhism is a Mahayana tradition found in **Japan**.

✣ This tradition emphasizes the worship of the **Buddha Amitabha**, who created the Pure Land.

✣ **Meditation** often involves the repetition of the name of Amitabha Buddha as a form of mantra.

Mahayana is a very varied school of Buddhism, in terms of its practice and imagery. Yet it is united by a shared concern to help all beings achieve enlightenment.

'You cannot travel the path until you have become the path itself.'
Siddartha Gautama

Zen Buddhism

One of the best-known schools of Mahayana Buddhism is **Zen**.

Once, while teaching, the Buddha is thought to have held up a flower. A monk, **Mahakasyapa**, correctly interpreted the significance of the flower. The Buddha was emphasizing a special teaching, which concentrated on **direct meditation experience** rather than book learning.

This teaching became the origin of **Ch'an Buddhism** in China, and later Zen Buddhism in Japan. The teaching was carried to China from India, by the southern Indian monk Bodhidharma.

> **'Zen is often defined by the verse attributed to Bodhidharma as "a special transmission outside the scriptural teachings".'**
>
> A. Koné

The Soto and Rinzai schools

Zen Buddhism assumes that when we recapture our Buddha nature, then we shall become enlightened. In Japan, the two main Zen schools are **Soto** and **Rinzai**.

As described in chapter 6, the main method for achieving enlightenment is meditation.

* In Soto Zen, the prime method is to calm the mind without **any** specific subject for meditation.
* In Rinzai Zen, the practitioners focus on a **koan**, or linguistic puzzle, which they have to try to solve.

> Zen has been very influential in the West, particularly in literature and philosophy.

Further reading

Armstrong, K. *Buddha* (London: Phoenix, 2002).

Carrithers, M. *The Buddha: A Very Short Introduction* (Oxford: Oxford University Press, 2001).

Conze, E. *Buddhism: A Short History* (Oxford: Oneworld, 2000).

Geaves, R. *Key Words in Buddhism* (London: Continuum, 2006).

Gethin, R. *The Buddhist Path to Awakening* (Oxford: Oneworld, 2001).

Klostermaier, K. K. *Buddhism: A Short Introduction* (Oxford: Oneworld, 1999).

Snelling, J. *The Buddhist Handbook: A Complete Guide to Buddhist Teaching and Practice* (London: Rider, 1998).

Strong, J. S. *The Buddha: A Short Biography* (Oxford: Oneworld, 2001).

References

Bell, S. 'Being creative with tradition: rooting Theravada Buddhism in Britain', *Journal of Global Buddhism*, 1 (2000), 1–23, p.15.

Erricker, C. *Buddhism* (London: Hodder Education, 2003), p.90.

Farrer-Halls, G. *The Buddha Book* (London: Godsfield, 2005), p.28.

Loy, D. R. 'Buddhism and poverty', *Contemporary Buddhism*, 2:1 (2001), 55–71, at p.56.

Freiberger, O. 'Profiling the sangha: institutional and non-institutional tendencies in early Buddhist teachings', *Marburg Journal of Religion*, 5:1 (2000), 1–12, at p.1.

Koné, A. 'Zen in Europe: a survey of the territory', *Journal of Global Buddhism*, 2 (2001), 139–61, at p.153.

Kulananda *Buddhism* (London: Thorsons, 2001), p. 26.

Lorentz, T. 'The dharma and the West: Can Buddhism survive consumerism?', *Contemporary Buddhism*, 2:2 (2001), 191–9, at p.193.

McDonald, T. J. 'Ameriyana: The Western Vehicle of the Buddha Dharma' *Intermountain West Journal of Religious Studies*, 2:1 (2010), 40–58, at p.41.

Sevilla, A. L. 'Founding human rights within Buddhism: exploring Buddha-Nature as an ethical foundation', *Journal of Buddhist Ethics*, 17 (2010), 212–50, at p.219.